I0162106

Victims of

Violent

Crime

By

Ted & Diana

Harrington

DEDICATION

This book is dedicated to the thousands of friends, relatives, acquaintances and caring people who have stood by our sides, supported us with their love, understanding and help over the past 26 years. We cannot name each and every person that was involved in this long ordeal, but our deep appreciation and heartfelt thanks is extended personally to each and every individual.

Our gratitude extends to the many detectives, police and law enforcement personnel that worked tirelessly on this crime. Without their continuous and outstanding dedication, this horrific crime would have gone unsolved.

A personal thanks specifically to two individuals, Stan Levco and Bob Pigman. Without their expertise, remarkable intelligence and undying ambition to seek justice for this crime, a guilty verdict would never have been concluded. In addition, the many personnel that assisted these two gentlemen in their efforts is greatly appreciated.

Words cannot express our feelings and the many years, Father Ted Temple, has stood by our sides with spiritual guidance. He has been a rock, a strong shoulder for my family and a personal friend.

We applaud all the reporters, editors and publishers that have accurately and extensively covered this story over the past 26 years; their drive was relentless and necessary to convey factual information to the public. We appreciate all forms of the media, the newspapers, TV, etc. for their years of coverage. There were hundreds of reporters, too numerous to mention, that were involved in this case. Each one is extended personal thanks from us.

There were specific media personnel that went beyond the realm of just reporters; Brad Byrd, Maureen Hayden and Anne Ryder. Mere coverage of this case was the furthest assignment in their minds. They not only became personally involved with this case but felt the sadness, the anger, the frustrations and shed many tears throughout their involvement. Their professional articles on the many sides to this story are greatly appreciated and their friendships are cherished.

I want to extend personal thank yous to Anne Seymour and Ellen Halbert. They introduced an avenue for me to platform my views on Victims Rights. They have helped me to become a strong voice for many victims of violent crime. This venue will be a continuing new chapter in my life.

This book is dedicated to my parents Lawrence and Dorothy Sahm. Most importantly, however, this book is dedicated to the Gilligan family; Pat, Theresa, Lisa and Greg. The memory of this loving family will always be present in many hearts. Diana & Ted Harrington

Table of Contents:

CHAPTER 1...

I am a Victim of Violent Crime
The Beginning, the Crime

Just before midnight, January 14th, 1980, the phone by our bedside rang. Ted, my husband, startled by the loud ring, grabbed it and turned on the light. I heard him say "What!" as he shot into a fully awakened state. "What?" he nearly screamed into the phone a second time. Something inside my stomach sank as I watched the color drain from his face".

His face became a stark, sickly white shade. I had never seen a look so devastating in my life. The look of utter desolation is one that I will never forget; a look of shock and complete disbelief. He listened quietly and as if totally defeated, softly murmured, "We are on our way".

Ted turned to me, his shoulders already sagging, and looked directly into my eyes, "We need to get to your parent's home. Pat and Theresa have been in an accident. They've been killed." He added nothing about the children.

I sat motionless. I couldn't even ask a coherent question. I vaguely remember hearing the words but not recognizing them. There was a roaring in my ears that made hearing, let alone speaking, nearly impossible.

We quickly and quietly dressed for the drive across town to my parent's home. I had not realized that Ted had only told me a part of the tragedy. He was not able to speak the unthinkable and I would not learn the extent of our loss for another 20 minutes.

Pulling up to my parent's house, I noticed a Sheriff's car parked in front of the house and numerous other police and official cars that were not familiar to the neighborhood. Ted and I entered the house. The first person I saw was Father Temple, our dear family friend and parish priest. I could see Dad and Mom in the background, both crying. The Sheriff came to me, his face very solemn and full of pain. I imagine it was taking every ounce of strength he had to maintain his

composure, especially with what he had just
witnessed.

He spoke softly and his voice cracked, "I am sorry
but Pat, Theresa, Lisa and Greg have been killed.
They are all gone." The pain it took to tell me was
seen in his eyes, quivering lips and his sunken
shoulders.

Once the words were spoken, I could hear myself
mumble almost in a whisper, "What! The kids? All
of them?"

"Yes, they are all gone?" he said, as his eyes welled
up with tears.

"You're wrong! This can't be true!" I screamed,
"No! No! No! This is a mistake!"

I was saying words, screaming loudly but not
making any sense. Just repeating myself and
looking at everyone's face. Nothing was penetrating
in my head, it was all just words. It was not real.
There was a roaring sound in my ears blocking all

sounds except my own shattered voice.

I thought I must wake up from this dream, but I knew I was already awake. It was real and it was really happening. "What happened? Was it an accident? Were they in their car? A fire? What?!"

As Father Ted held my hand and the Sheriff placed his hand on my shoulder, the Sheriff told me. "There was a terrible accident, they were shot. A burglar broke into the house and shot them."

This was even harder to comprehend. I was stunned; it was just not making sense. What I was hearing and what was going into my ears and trying to connect to my brain was just not working correctly.

Again I said, "What? I don't understand. Shot? All of them? Killed? They are gone?"

The Sheriff repeated himself, "Yes, they were all shot. We believe a burglar broke into the house and shot them."

I had understood what he had said but I had chosen to block the words out the first time. My brain and my heart had simply shut down... it was all just words.

I glanced at everyone's face. They all had that look. It was the same pale, white sickly look with no color.   The same look that Ted had just a few minutes ago when he answered the phone. There was nothing but a blank look. A horrid look, a look of disbelief. A look that the whole world had been torn apart. We were all in shock. We occupied the same space...we shared an agonizing suffering and loss...it was a look of shock that would be with us for all time. It was a look that told you your life would never be the same.

At that exact moment I felt something inside me break. It was as if someone had taken a lovely crystal glass and crushed it with one tight squeeze. Shattering it into tiny fragments. My entire body was thousands of slivers of glass that had broken with three simple words, "They are gone."

Something replaced the Diana that was there at that moment with a person that was different in every respect. I have never hurt so much in my entire life. My heart was beating too fast and had climbed into my throat. My entire sense of being was falling apart. I was shaking uncontrollably. It hurt to breathe. It hurt to think. My head ached with the uncertainty and the pain was unbearable. Someone ripped my entire life apart in just seconds. **Gone...Gone. Gone was all I could imagine.**

I quickly went to Mom and Dad and while sharing our tears and sorrow, the Sheriff said, "I would advise you to call anyone that needs to be notified. Anyone that you feel should not hear this over the news, call them. This will be making the morning headlines. The state police will be notifying the news media around 3:15AM."

<u>At that moment,</u>
<u>I Became a Victim of Violent Crime.</u>

My family; my only sister, brother-in-law, niece and nephew, had entered and surprised a burglar while he was ransacking and burglarizing their home. The perpetrator tied them up, tortured them, shot all of them in the head and beat my brother-in-law with barbells so badly a closed casket was inevitable.

This was my family....my thirty year old sister Theresa and brother-in-law Pat, my five year old niece Lisa and four year old nephew Greg **(The Patrick Gilligan Family).**

This crime was committed in 1980 and the criminal, Donald Ray Wallace Jr., sat on death row for 25 years claiming his innocence.

Wallace was one of the longest death row inmates in Indiana. This crime still stands as being one of the most heinous in Indiana.

To the knowledge of the Indiana Attorney General, in March of 2005, this was the longest

appeals process on the record books.

On March 10th, 2005, the sentence was carried out .... Donald Ray Wallace Jr. was executed for the cold blooded vicious murders of four innocent people....
25 years after the crime!

The uphill battle had just begun. Along this long and painful journey were days and nights of highs and lows with the highs too shallow and the lows a frightening depth to climb above.

It is not unusual with the sudden and violent loss of those so dear to us to feel alone, desolate and lost. I was in shock and I was the most vulnerable in my life. It is pain and agony no one should endure and it lasts for an eternity.

It is the same for everyone when they become a victim of violent crime... shock and disbelief. In such a brief second all is changed.

At that moment my life changed. I had been a 27

year old, newly married, career oriented and robust-on-life individual. I was supposed to live happily ever after with my new husband and all my loved ones until we grew old and grey. We would look back at our lives with laughter and glee. When we felt our children were wise and ready, we would pass the torch for them to carry on in the same tradition.

It was not supposed to happen this way. Nothing prepared me to bury four members of my family, clean up a crime scene, settle an estate, listen to a trial, write to criminals, deal with the crowds and answer all the questions. My education did not teach me what to do as I saw my Mom and Dad, friends, other family, acquaintances and community fall apart and suffer such pain.

I simply was not meant to be a spokesperson for my family's deaths nor was I suppose to fight to make sure my family's name remained first instead of the criminal.

I did not intend, in my fairy tale lifetime, to become

adept at the process of death row appeals or victims rights.

I had not asked nor had I chose to become a victim of violent crime. My future and everyone's future that was touched by this senseless crime did not include this tragedy.

However, just like any victim of violent crime who is drop kicked into this situation, no one asks a heinous crime, such as this, to be part of their life.

Violent crimes happen everyday and with each violent crime a victim is created. Each victim struggles day by day trying to make sense of such a cruel trick that has been thrown at them.

Why were we cheated out of the lives we had planned and why were our loved ones singled out and their lives taken so abruptly?

We search for others to understand what we are going through and for them to know, just an ounce, of the agony and pain we feel.

We know that violent crimes occur every day.
However, they were not supposed to happen to us.
Right?

So, what do we do now? How do we cope? What
questions do we ask? Where do we find the
answers? How do we go on?

It took many years after the crime to learn how to
cope and survive, day to day, minute by minute. I
also learned how I felt, and how others in my
family, along with friends, neighbors and the entire
community, felt. This crime took away an entire
communities innocence as it had taken mine. It was
years before I could sort out these feelings. I finally
understood how this heinous crime affected so
many lives and how it changed my life.

It was and still is a long tough road that we travel.
It will always be with me and will always haunt me.

I am not a doctor, a lawyer, an expert nor a
magician. I can't offer a pill for this horrible

nightmare to be gone for you. I do, however, feel your pain and I do understand what you are facing. I want to offer you hope for the future and maybe some comfort in the present. I want to share with you the long journey and the path I have taken. What I have learned from this long trek.

I am living proof that your life will continue once you learn to live one day at a time. I hope that I can offer some help and insight for you as a fellow victim of violent crime.

There are many victims of violent crime and we are in the same situation as you. We are all struggling together to make sense of these crimes. We are all working for the same goal.

Among the victims that I have encountered I have found one common thread. We have the same questions and the same reasons for being heard. We want our loved ones to be remembered and for there to be a purpose to these meaningless crimes. We also want others to understand the pain and what we go through.

I have found fellow victims to have big ears to listen and big hearts that understand. Their doors are always open to lend help and strength. We all stand alone yet are really not alone at all.

Hopefully this book will help others to understand our world and also help victims in moving forward.

CHAPTER 2

The Inevitable Questions,
"Why?" "How Could This Happen?"

The first two questions that uttered my lips after this crime were, "Why?" and, "How could this happen?" To this day, 27 years after the crime, I still search for the answers to these questions.

When I was in college, taking Psychology 101, my professor gave us a strange final exam. He turned around to the blackboard and simply wrote, WHY?

Most students were writing pages upon pages of answers, while others, looking out into space, pondered the meaning of this word. A couple students walked out of class completely perplexed with how to finish this semester exam with the one word question. I'm sure they felt they were going to fail since they had no idea how to answer it.

After the class ended and every student had handed in their papers, several students asked what the professor was looking for.

"What is the answer to your question? " They asked. With arrogance and sharpness to his voice, the professor simply said there were two correct answers to the question. The answers were, "Why not," and "Because".

He continued by comparing it to a small child that continuously asks, "Why?" You answer, more than likely, to the "why" questions with complex replies. The more why's a child has the more answers you come up with and the more complex the answers.

Most often it is never the correct answer that a child wants to hear. And so it continues, the never ending stream of "whys" from this child.

You will finally arrive at a final answer of, "Just because," or "Well, why not". You cannot think of any additional explanations or elaborate reasons. Your last response to the child is as simple as there are no more answers to the questions.

Why's are never answered with one simple

statement. There are always continuous answers
that piggyback the initial why. You finally get to a
crossroad with no real answers.

Those two answers are probably the best answers
we will ever receive when asking why a crime
happens.

I have searched for 27 years for final answers to
these questions, "Why my family?" "Why were
they killed?" "Why the children" … and I have
found nothing to answer my questions.

It is unjust, unfair and completely incomprehensible
that these violent, heinous crimes continue and it is
so unjust for the victims. But it is part of our world
and out of the goodness in our hearts and nature, we
cannot figure it out.

We ask, "Why did this happen? Why my loved
ones? Why was I the recipient of this crime?" But
none of us have any answers nor will there be, in
most circumstances, any final definitive answers.

Maybe there is a bigger picture that we cannot see or maybe it is just a game of roulette that ends with the victims having the chosen number.

I want to believe that there is a better and higher reason that certain people were picked to be in these situations.

Possibly there is some life purpose that we have not found yet from these experiences. Maybe these questions, or at least, better answers will be answered in due time.

Until that time, however, answers to our questions can only be compared to the small child' questions. We can go on continuously asking our initial question, "Why" over and over until we can't answer anymore why's and are led to the final answer, Why not or Because.

Most importantly, is that we understand there are no reasons why.

How could this happen?

My mother always had this question, "How could this happen?" She had such a close relationship and a very strong "vibe" with her daughter. She would, as if with ESP, know when the phone was going to ring prior to it actually ringing. She knew when something was wrong, by instinct, or when something was bothering my sister.

She would, over the remaining years of her life, ask herself, "Why didn't I have those instincts when this crime was happening?" "How could it have happened without my feeling those same feelings that I normally had? Why couldn't I feel that she was in danger? Why didn't I hear her crying?"

My only response to her was that my sister was more than likely not thinking of anyone but her husband, children and herself. Maybe, if there is a strong energy, something like instinct or ESP, this vibration was not directed in my mother's way.

In response to her question why didn't I know, I often told my mother, "Would it have made a difference?" Even, in as much as, we would have liked to thwart this crime, nothing could have prevented it. Most crimes happen so fast there is little time to stop or prevent any danger from happening.

Were we even meant to stop them? If there is a "plan" that we are not aware of, we could not stop this fatal destiny even if we wanted.

There will always be questions and these questions will continue throughout the years. Maybe someday you will have your answers. But for every victim of violent crime there seems to be questions that simply don't have answers.

It is easier said than done not to dwell on the Why's or How's and to simply say there is a power far beyond our comprehension that holds the entire picture. I know it is not much consolation but if you can find a way to let go of these questions, the path will be much easier for you.

For you to beat yourself up over these unanswered

questions is something that was not meant to be. It is not healthy for you and will not change anything that is in the present.

Furthermore, if you had all the answers to your initial why's and how's, wouldn't there be a hundred more waiting in line to be answered?

CHAPTER 3...

The cycle of

Hate, Anger & Guilt

I believe, other than shock, my first two reactions and feelings were anger and hate. I hated this monster that killed my family. How could anyone be so cruel and insensitive? How could any human being commit such a heinous, cold blooded crime? How could anyone murder innocent people and especially innocent children?

This anger and hatred consumed me. I held, deep inside, my anger and disgust at this "thing" called a human. If he could only undergo the same torture that he inflicted on my family. Could he be killed four times?

"What would I do to him if I could get my hands on him?" My whole being wanted to harm him. From my fingers to my toes, I could feel the anger, the hatred and the disgust I felt towards this person. How could anyone take another's life? And in such a cruel manner.

When I thought of my actions or dreamed of what I would do, I would get to the point of hurting him and I would immediately stop. I couldn't do it. I stopped at the point of cruelty or causing him pain.

I felt guilt that I wanted to inflict harm on another human being. The guilt then became as overwhelming as the hate and anger. I knew it was wrong to hate so much. I knew it was wrong to want to hurt but there was very little control over my emotions until I actually faced, with my visions, of what I'd do.

Was I just as low as this person and his actions? I was reminded, by my faith, that he was a human being and a creature of God. However, I could not see an ounce of good or any salvation in his soul. Nor could I see any reason why God created such a monster. I still, however, could not deny he was human.

I found myself in a circle...anger, hatred, guilt...anger, hatred, guilt. I simply could not go through the rest of my life chasing this vicious circle. It was useless and frustrating. It was the center of my stress and it was making me sick.

Most victims, I have talked with, are caught up in the same circle. Their beliefs and their goodness are questioned by their feelings of hatred towards the criminal. Their losing loved ones to such a senseless crime and murder are easily channeled towards this criminal rather than looking at the actions of the criminal. Trust me; it is hard to distinguish between the two.

It was not easy nor did it happen overnight. I spent many years just spinning around and around in this circle and it seemed like there was no way off. If I had any chance of getting off this merry-go-round, I needed to change. If there was any chance of me regaining my sanity and my emotions, I needed to change.

I realized that every human being, no matter how low and disgusting they seem, has worth. Their actions and reactions are deep seeded. These beliefs and ways of life have been cultivated and nurtured for years. We may never know why people act as they do but it certainly is not going to change simply by hating, voicing anger or showing ones temper. It simply does not accomplish anything.

Since this was a useless circle, I tried to look at the crime and criminal differently. If I were able to physically hurt this criminal, as I truly wanted to, would it make a difference in <u>my</u> life or ease my pain? Would it have changed the lives of others or helped others in similar situations? Would it lessen the grief I was feeling? Would it turn back time and bring my family back to me? The definitive answer was, "No".   The only thing it would have accomplished is harming another person, along with hurting others in the process.

Other than instant gratification for the exploding of my anger, my heart of hearts said this would not prove anything.

I came to a point where I needed to expend my energy on more useful purposes or I would die being hateful and full of anger.

I became indifferent to the idea of hurting him and started to direct my anger at the crime and the circumstances of the crime.

I came to the conclusion that it was OK to hate and to be angry but not at another human being. I hated the situation that this criminal placed me in and what he did. Whatever led him to kill four innocent people, I would never forget, nor would I forgive how that moment of rage changed the lives of so many.

I started to channel my anger and hatred toward something that could be changed and not on someone that could not be changed. It was tangible results that I could measure and see. My anger, frustration and hatred were switching from the criminal to the crime and I found situations that I had the possibility of changing.

If somehow I could help correct laws that would make the government proactive instead of reactive, wouldn't that be a better way of expending my energy. If someone, by chance, listened, could I make a difference?

I could be angry with the way victims are treated and try to change the system. Maybe if I spoke loud enough I could prevent a crime such as this from happening again. If people, prior to a crime, would understand what great depths of pain they inflict on so many people would they think twice about a life of crime. Could this prevent future crimes?

My voice was small and polite at first but once people started to listen and agree, it became loud and confident. Not that I have set the world afire, but I have made my opinions clear and precise. Even if it is baby steps, it is helping me find some reason for this crime and a purpose for me being a victim of violent crime.

If you can focus on the victims and the crime, not the criminal, maybe situations such as these can be prevented or changed for someone else. Your anger and frustration will be directed to a better place and a place where you can possibly see change for your efforts.

I have known many victims that have started memorial funds, scholarships and worked with the present laws in order to prevent future crime or to help others.

Find an avenue, whether it be a law, a rule, a fund or a direction. If you don't feel comfortable being an activist for a purpose, find somewhere else to channel your feelings. A hobby, a charity, work, art, education…and the list continues.

It can be something small or something larger than life but let it be the avenue for your anger and hatred. Find something that will make a difference in the way you feel about the crime, your loved ones and yourself. Something you feel good about and something that makes a difference in your world.

Do not dismiss your feelings of anger and hatred. You certainly do not want to minimize your emotions but rather redirect your anger. These negative feelings can be changed to a positive force to be reckoned with. It is so easy to spend your life in hatred, anger and unhappiness if you let yourself be drawn into that black hole.

Remember, so vividly, that life is short and now more than ever make the most of your life in a positive direction.

Chapter 4

The Loss of Your Loved One,
"How can I deal with it?"

Grieving the loss of a victim of violent crime is not a luxury for the victims left behind. Dealing with shock, financial worries, anger, the media and many issues that are thrown in your direction does not give you the time or the energy to dwell on your loss.

The death of a loved one is hard to deal with on its own much less with police, investigators and the eyes of the community on you. The grieving process seems stalled with everything strange and unnatural thrown at you and your brain is having a hard time comprehending the tragedy.

It is very hard to realize that a violent crime has *really* happened to your loved one. You wish you could wake up from this nightmare and all would be back to normal. Not only do you miss your loved one terribly but you have a hard time dealing with the way in which they were taken from your life. So unexplainable, so unnecessary and so cruel. Not only do you feel the loss but everyone that is touched by the crime has the same feeling.

I can remember the community mourning my family's deaths and how it touched their lives. How after 25 years, the pain still lingered as they were unable to let go and continue with their lives. Somehow many stayed in that same moment and could recall it with precise recollection. It is surprising how crimes such as these affect many people in many ways.

The grieving process is very different for everyone and each individual experiences it differently. It is very important that you accept the process and move to a plateau that you feel safe, secure and a place you can deal with your loss. It is easy to remain in the same moment in time and not move on as it is sometimes too incredibly hard to deal with. A minister, priest, professional or someone you can talk with helps tremendously in dealing with your grief.

Healing only comes with time and unlike the

saying, time heals all wounds, the feeling of your loss will be with you as long as you can remember. Hopefully, though, time will help you work through your grief and continue the healing process.

Time also allows you to resolve the many feelings that are associated with a violent crime and put them into perspective. It is definitely not an easy path but one that needs to be traveled.

In the depths of my agony and despair, something inside guided me, helped me and listened to my pain.

I know that in my darkest days, if I would listen, I would be able to find that inner strength that comes from deep within. I would like to think it was from the strength that my family gave to me. Even though they were no longer here in body, I could find them helping me along and as if taking my hand and leading me through a deep maze to the end of the tunnel.

There were many days when I thought, "There is no

way I can continue," As soon as this feeling tried to take over, I would suddenly feel a peace, a full feeling or I was reminded of their existence or spirit. I knew they were close and I only needed to listen to that inner strength in order to feel them.

Anyone who has lost a loved one can relate to this and I have no explanations for it. This overwhelming feeling helps you get from point A to point B when your own will can't make it.

Over the years I called upon their help and they were always there. Guiding me and taking me in the direction I needed to go. Their guidance and strength let me know I would be OK and I would be able to continue.

I love telling this story, as I know it was not by accident that my sister wanted to let me know she was still with me. In the first few days after the murders, I was totally lost. Literally I was spinning in circles. I was in shock and deep agony. My only reason for living was to protect my parents and to keep them from as much pain as I could. To look back on these days now, I don't know how I continued or how I accomplished the tasks that were at hand. I only understood there were "things" that needed to be done and these "things" were in my hands.

Three days before my sister, Theresa, was murdered we went shopping. It was a lovely day with my mother, my sister, my niece and nephew. We happened upon a beautiful brass plate with two pewter doves in the center and words written on the top, ***"We are one love Forever"***. My sister and I both reached for the plate at the same time.

I exclaimed, "I simply love it," however, it was in my sister's hands before I could even utter the words. I thought for certain she would say, "You can have it."

Instead she said, "This is perfect for Pat. I have the perfect place for it and I'll keep it till our 11th anniversary". At that moment, I distinctly remember her saying, "Pat and I are so lucky, there's really so few people who ever find the kind of love we have."

I remember saying, "Ted and I know that love and he will truly love this. I can give it to him for our 1 month anniversary". We had just been married on Jan 4th. (The murders were on Jan. 14th)

Smiling, I reached into her basket, took the plate and placed it in mine. She laughed and we continued our shopping as Mom glanced out of the corner of her eye at both of us and the kids just giggled. I guess they all were wondering how this would end.

After several minutes, I noticed the plate was no longer in my basket. I looked into my sister's basket to see she had it covered by a set of towels. Needless to say, it did not take me but a couple minutes to be sneaky enough to regain the plate in my basket under some items I planned to purchase.

When we went to the checkout, I was very happy that she had relented and left it in my basket. We paid for our items and then proceeded to the car.

I noticed when I got home I had paid for the plate but it was not in any of my packages. I immediately called Theresa and she chuckled, "I'll pay you back for it." I remember thinking how on earth did she end up with the plate. I was genuinely glad she got the plate and thought it would be a perfect gift for Pat. That was the last time I saw and talked to my sister.

After the murders, it was time to go to my sister's home and pick out the funeral outfits for all four, Pat, Theresa, Lisa and Greg. It was, at that time, one of the lowest days of my life and I thought there was no way it could get any lower. I thought to myself how would I be able to do this without breaking down completely.

As I approached the house, covered in yellow crime tape, it did not look at all like the house that just a few days earlier was filled with love and happiness.

The FBI investigators, police, lab personnel, etc were still combing the scene for leads and evidence. Two FBI personnel followed me throughout the house making sure there was no evidence disturbed from the scene.

I went from bedroom to bedroom selecting the children's clothes. I entered Pat & Theresa's bedroom, opened the closet and proceeded to find a particular dress that I thought would be perfect and was Mom's favorite on Theresa. In the closet I easily recognized the rose-colored dress along with Pat's best suit, shirt and a tie. I needed to select shoes for them both but I was so powerfully drawn to look on the upper shelf of the closet. I don't know why....but I felt as if I was being willed to look. It was an unsettling feeling because it seemed to come from within me.

I moved several stacks of clothes and boxes from the back, sandwiched under two planks of shelving and tucked neatly in the far back corner, where no one would ever find it, I found the bag from our shopping trip on Saturday.

I will never to this day understand what possessed me to look under the boxes, shelving and clothes.

There would have been no way, even if I had my chance to search for it, would I have ever found it on my own. Theresa had hidden this so perfectly. I'm sure she was keeping it from Pat or anyone ever finding it.

I opened the bag and there it was, the beautiful brass plate we had both wanted.... *__"We are one love forever"__*...... I knew that Theresa wanted me to find it.

I felt that she knew this was one of the hardest situations I had ever encountered. Going from one of the happiest days to one of the saddest days, I needed to remember the joy she had brought to my life. As I held the plate in my hand, I felt her warmth and spirit.

I knew from that moment that I only needed to call and she would be there.

Many strange and wonderful occurrences happened in the years after the murders that I nor anyone else can explain, however, I do know that if you listen to your heart you will find your loved ones spirit.

The memories of all the laughter, smiles, tears, joy and happiness that you shared cannot be erased by their deaths. It is only a short distance away from you. It rests in your heart and you only need to call upon them to find your loved ones still there.

Some of the victims I have talked with find writing letters, talking out loud in conversations, visiting places that were favorite to both of you, seeing old friends and so on, are helpful. The feeling of being close to your loved one in a familiar setting or just a conversation is very comforting. It can bring back the loving memories you shared and their wonderful life with you.

Some victims have found it comforting to write goodbyes since that deed was stolen from them by the crime. Some write letters when a certain event seems too lonely without them. They explain the entire event as if they were there to share the day with them.

I have talked to victims that purchase Birthday
cards, Anniversary cards and so on and place them
on their gravesites.   There was one that purchased
gifts and then donated them to charity. She said she
found pleasure in knowing someone else enjoyed
the gift.

No matter what avenue you find that gives you
comfort, <u>do it</u>. Call upon their spirit often,
especially when you need them and you will find
the strength to continue. Do what it takes to make
yourself feel comforted, write letters, talk out loud,
buy gifts, etc... Do not think it is silly or crazy, just
do it!

Yes, you will find it difficult, almost unbearable,
not to have them present to hug and kiss but they
will always be with you in your heart and mind.

CHAPTER 5

The Bills Are Overwhelming,
"Can I get help?"

The average person does not understand the enormous financial decisions and burdens that are involved in the aftermath of a violent crime. From funeral costs to medical expenses, to liquidating estates, to clean up, none are reasonable or expected expenditures.

If there is a crime scene, it is normally the responsibility of the victims to clean up, throw away or dispose of the mess. This can mount to enormous expenses.

When there is an investigated scene, everyone seems to play havoc on the premises. Not only do you have the damage from a burglar and the struggles from the victims but you have to clean after the investigators. (Police, forensics, laboratory, coroner, etc.) Needless to say, they have to do a thorough job but are quite messy. This clean up can be overwhelming and quite costly.

Normal maintenance of any property that is left is another financial burden that is not expected. Expenses for normal upkeep, utilities and mortgage or rent payments can stress anyone. You wonder how it will be paid.

Most often extra time off from your work is needed or required. An extended leave of absence might not be offered by your employer or time off not available. In fact, I have heard of several victims that have lost their jobs due to the time that was needed away from their work in order to accomplish small tasks that are associated with the crime and extended grieving. Most workplaces give the normal 3 days off for a death. This is simply not enough time to recover from the sudden deaths of your loved ones, much less accomplish everything that is needed from the aftermath of a violent crime.

I know that when the murders of my family occurred, we were all devastated. I was unable to return to work immediately and Ted, my husband was required to go back after just three days off. We had so much to deal with; the estate, trial, normal upkeep of the house, clean up, etc., that it was very difficult to take the time off and still work. It took years for us to liquidate the estate and the trial took almost 3 years till its culmination. We were grateful that Ted's job was one where he could adjust his schedule. However, it meant he worked longer days to get off for just a few hours.

In addition, if you are in need of a mental health practitioner sometimes visits are not covered under normal insurance policies. Visits can last for weeks and months with follow-ups for years. This is a gigantic expense if your insurance does not help.

The above unexpected costs are just a small handful of expenses that add stress for the victims and break their pocketbooks. Not only do you have to deal with the loss of your loved one, but to deal with all these unexpected debts can lead to stress on top of stress.

To alleviate some of this financial trauma, there are several victim assistance programs that are available for victims of violent crime.

VOCA is the Victims of Crime Act. It is a federal
law that provides financial assistance to support a
variety of services and activities to assist victims of
crime. This act was enacted by Congress in 1984
and was made permanent in 1988. The money
comes from various federal criminal fines,
forfeitures, assessments and penalties. None of the
money used by VOCA comes from taxpayer
appropriations. VOCA grants to each State crime
victim compensation programs.

Some of the expenses or funds available that might
be reimbursed to victims of violent crime are:
Medical and medical-related expenses, fees for
counseling or therapy for the victim and his/her
family members. Costs incurred as a result of the
victim's participation in support or therapy groups.
Expenses for medications that doctors may
prescribe for victims to help ease their trauma
following a crime. Outpatient mental health
treatment or counseling.
Funeral and burial expenses. Costs associated with
burials, i.e. caskets, cemetery plots, memorial

services, etc.

Expenses for travel to plan and/or attend funerals.

Wage or income loss.

Support, loss for legal dependents of a deceased or injured victim.

Wage loss for the parent or legal guardian of a minor victim who is hospitalized or dies as a direct result of a crime.

Job retraining.

Medically necessary renovation or retrofitting of a home or vehicle for a person permanently disabled as a result of the crime.

Home security installation or improvements if the crime occurred in the victim's home. Costs of replacing locks, changing security devices, etc.

In-patient psychiatric hospitalization costs under dire or exceptional circumstances.

Relocation expenses

Crime scene cleanup, if a victim dies as a result of a crime in a residence.

Expenses related to child or elder care when victims have to testify in court.

Fees incurred in changing banking or credit card accounts.

To be eligible for compensation, a person must be a victim of a qualifying crime involving physical injury, threat of physical injury or death and meet the criteria for your State. Each State is different and each has certain requirements. Certain family members or other loved ones who suffer an economic loss resulting from an injury to, or death of, a victim of a crime may also be eligible for compensation.

*contact your local assistance program for specific qualifying requirements, criteria and reimbursement funds that are available.

According to NOVA, National Organization for Victim's Assistance, the easiest way to find out if there is a victim assistance program in your local law enforcement agency is to ask the officer who takes the crime report. Ask if their agency has such a program. Ask the officer to contact the victim assistance program, or ask for the phone number of the program so you can contact the program directly.

If there is no victim assistance program in your local law enforcement agency, ask the officer for the community-based referrals.

You can also contact the local prosecutor's office. Ask to speak to a victim advocate, who can either provide services directly, or may refer you to a different program. If the offender is arrested for the crime, the victim assistance program in the prosecutor's office should be able to help you as the case is prosecuted in court or if it is handled in some other way.

You will need to do some research to see what is available to you and what programs will apply to your individual circumstances.

You will also need to document your expenses for reimbursement. Some of the documentation that is

needed might be… wage statements from your
employer for unpaid time as a result of the crime,
injuries or involvement in the justice processes,
workers compensation claims, copies of bills for
services related to the crime, receipts for purchased
items or services, documentation of the value for
stolen property, photos of valuables that were stolen
or damaged, copies from law enforcement that aid
in the recovery of stolen property as well as
recovered damaged items, applications and checks
of received victim compensations funds, insurance
claims between the victim and the insurance
company. In other words you will need any receipts,
checks, copies or documentation that you may have
in order to aid in the reimbursement of stolen or
damaged items, fees and so on that are associated
directly with the crime.

Each and every victim has the right to receive help
from the government when they have encountered
such violent crimes. Not only do they have the
right but they have the need for this assistance.

One of my platforms for victim's rights is the continuance of these assistance programs for victims. This is the only federal grant program supporting direct assistance services to victims of all types of crimes. There are over 4,400 local programs that now depend on VOCA assistance funds to provide services to nearly 4 million crime victims…and the compensation to victims continues to increase.

After a 10 year decline of violent crimes, there is now an increase thus creating more and more victims of violent crime.

Here are just a few mind boggling statistics: Benefits that were received by victims and their families totaled $427 million in 2005 and compensation nearly doubled what it had been just seven years ago.

These programs paid $16.8 million for forensic sexual assault exams, which was nearly a 50% increase since 2003. Victims of child abuse

comprised 18% of the recipients of compensation
and domestic violence victims were 20% of all adult
victims compensated. Medical expenses were 53%
of all payments: economic support for lost wages
for injured victims, and for lost support in
homicides, comprised 19% of the total; 11% of total
payments were went for funeral bills; and 8% went
toward health counseling for crime victims. *stats
taken from the National Association of Crime Victim Association
Boards.

These are staggering amounts that comprise just a
portion of the compensation that is awarded to
victims of violent crime. Without this financial
support, a victim would be financially burdened
with out of pocket expenses that could soon
debilitate their credit.

Recently in a vote of 395/34, Congress adopted the
Poe/Costa/Moore amendment to the Commerce,
Justice and Science appropriations, thus increasing
the VOCA cap. This will keep the 2008 assistance
grants at the 2007 levels of need.

Unfortunately, the need for victim assistance is

growing.

This program doesn't use taxpayer money; VOCA
funding is money seized from criminals. It is
logical that money from offenders should go to
assist those who are victims of crime.

Over 4,400 victim service agencies in every state
and every district depend upon VOCA funding for
essential victim services, such as emergency
shelters, counseling, legal advocacy, and assistance
participating in the criminal justice system. This
includes victims of domestic violence, sexual
assault, child abuse, elder abuse, survivors of
homicide victims and drunken driving crashes.
Hundreds of thousands of victims were provided
financial assistance through VOCA grants to State
crime victim compensation programs.

VOCA was enacted after my family's murders so
we were unable to request or receive any financial
help or assistance. It is important to continue this
assistance for all victims. My family and I were left
with no financial or medical reimbursements when

we were in need. If this reverts back to the way it was in 1980, many victims will be in the same situation.

Make sure you voice your opinion, as a victim of violent crime, for the continuance of this program for all victims.

It is not only a lifesaver for victims, I believe, it is due to all victims of violent crime.

Chapter 6
Confronting the Criminal,
The Need to Know

At one point you might feel the need to confront the criminal that did this heinous crime. Not only for answers but to voice your feelings. You may have many questions to ask about the crime and your loved one. You also might want to get some feelings off your chest.

Most victims are haunted by wanting to know exactly what happened. What were the last moments like for my loved one? What did they go through? It is sad to depend on a criminal but only the victim and the criminal know those answers.

If the criminal was found, only he/she knows that answer. Whether they will admit, lie or deny the crime, that is up to them. However, you still would like to know and want to ask. Somehow it still haunts you to want to hear the story.

For 12 years, I went through horrible nightmares of what had happened in those last minutes before the murders. I knew by the forensics report, trial and murder scene that it was a struggle but I needed to know what happened.

I wanted to confront this criminal about that night. I also wanted to vent. I wanted to let him know what I had been through in the 12 years after the murders. I wanted him to know what my Mom and Dad had been through and what pain this crime had caused the rest of the family, our friends and our community. I was frightened by what I might hear but I still wanted to know and still wanted to ask. I wanted that option of at least asking or letting him know how I felt.

I contacted his attorney and after a long talk about the case, along with how I felt about the circumstances, I found out the criminal surprisingly had wanted to write to someone from my family.

Laws that protect victims made it impossible for him to contact any members of the family. In order for a criminal to contact the victim's family, they must have the family's permission. I gave my permission to receive his letter which, in turn, started a series of letters back and forth.

At first I did not know what he had to say but I was certainly interested.

Wallace's attorney called me about a week later and said she had a letter from him and she would forward it to me.   I received her letter with these instructions…

"I am enclosing the letter that Donald Ray Wallace Jr. wrote to you. If you want to write back to him, you can either send your letter through me or send it directly to him. He seems to understand your legitimate anger and hatred, and is prepared to hear you share your anger with him. If he says anything in his letter that offends or irritates you, you need to let him know."

After reading this introduction, my blood was boiling. I was again angered, scared, nervous and had feelings I was certain no one should feel towards another human. I knew that if he irritated me I was certain to let him know. How could he possibly understand how I felt? How could he ever feel the depths of my anger and hurt?

Inside the attorney's letter was a white envelope. A white sealed envelope. I knew his letter was inside. Did I want to open it? Did I really want to hear from him? After all this time, I was reluctant to open it. I knew however if I did not read it I would never know his intent.

I opened the envelope. The letter was written on a single sheet of college rule paper. It had been neatly folded into three sections. The letter was hand printed in black ink....

"Dear Ms Harrington,

This is the most difficult letter I have ever written. I don't know what I could possibly say to make you feel better.
I can't know how much pain the loss of Theresa,

Gregory, Lisa and Patrick gives you. I can only guess by imagining how I would feel if someone senselessly took away from me forever my closest sister. I don't think I could ever forgive someone for that.

Death row gives you hours and hours with nothing to do but look back on your life and to realize what grief you left in your wake. And so I have wondered many times how your mother and father felt to give birth to a baby girl, to protect and nurture her, to see her develop her own unique personality, to see her go to proms, to see her graduate high school, to see her marry and give birth to two beautiful children...and then to have that taken by reckless idiots whose petty want was money for drugs. And how must you have felt to lose your sister and her family for nothing - for no meaningful reason? I hate myself when I think these thoughts, and even I have no forgiveness for what I did on January 14, 1980.

I believe that I deserve to be executed. And I hope my death will bring peace and healing to all of you whom I have hurt. I am sorry from the center of my soul for the pain I have caused you.

Sincerely, Donald Wallace

I reread the letter. It echoed in my head...he cannot find the words to express... I counted up the I's that were in this letter and realized that this letter was simply how <u>he</u> felt. Not how <u>we</u> felt, not what we had endured but if this were him, how he would feel. Regardless of how much he wanted me to feel his sorrow, it was somehow not coming across.

I tried to remember the stories that he had told, his lies and not to forget he was a sociopath and compulsive liar. He was considered not the normal criminal and had an IQ of 147. He had read over 5,000 books, was well versed in law and was an excellent manipulator. Was he trying to manipulate me? And <u>perhaps he hoped to make me a convert with his words</u>.

However, he had said the words and his words were well selected. Should I believe him, was he truthful? Did he really mean it? Was there remorse? I was confused and quite frankly more confused than before I read the letter. I needed additional answers.

Ted was reassuring when I mentioned I wanted to write him back. I wanted to write a letter discussing the way I felt. I sat down that evening and wrote from my heart. I tried to hold nothing back. I wanted him to know exactly how I felt and that I deserved to know exactly what happened on January 14th, 1980.

My hands flew across the keys as I started typing.......

July 28, 1992
Donald Wallace,

I received your letter. I too find it hard to express in words what I feel and have lived with in the past 12 1/2 years. I feel, however, this letter is important. Important maybe to you but VERY important to me. You may read it or you may toss it, as I do not know if you really care about my feelings. I hope somewhere in this letter you will find that I too am a prisoner and have an understanding of how it feels being trapped behind bars. Hopefully, this letter will explain to you what bars and what prison I have been in.

As I stated, you may read this letter and you may choose not to read it. I'm sure you will not enjoy a majority of parts but it could prove to be an understanding you need to know. You may feel the rage, anger, disgust, frustration and the tremendous grief, sorrow and hurt that has been with me at least 4-5 times per day for 12 1/2 years. Everyday when I think of my family I think of you and wonder why. I still find it impossible to comprehend why.

You do not understand that when you took my sister, my brother-in-law, my niece and nephew you took my life also. The night I found out about the murders I no longer existed as I did before. We are not that much apart in age and my life prior was one where I could smile and laugh. I have not laughed or smiled in 12 1/2 years without feeling guilty that I am alive and my family is dead. I was robbed of my twenties and thirties because I had to grow up fast to take care of my mother and father,

*to protect them from a lot of grief. I learned quickly
what it was like to pick out four caskets, walk in my
sisters home and select four sets of clothing for the
funeral, how to plan for a mass funeral, how to sell
all of my sister and brother-in-laws belongings that
I knew they treasured, how to donate my niece and
nephews prized toys and to throw out their
paintings and drawings. I also grew up fast as I
scrubbed my family's blood off the walls and
cleaned up the brutal site where I could only
imagine pleadings for life or of little voices crying
for mommy and daddy existed.*

*Prior to this incident I was able to love
unconditionally my husband of only 10 days, our
wedding was Jan 4, 1980, and the reception was at
my sister's home. I found there will always be
apart of me that no one will ever touch, deep inside.
I keep it to myself because I never, never want to
hurt like that again. My whole being aches with a
hurt that is unbearable. It has not stopped and it
now, today, is the same feeling as it was then. I just
need to close my eyes to hear the phone ring and
the other end saying please go to your parent's*

house there has been an accident. It feels as it did then.

I so looked forward to one day making my sister and brother-in-law an aunt and uncle, as well as, the children cousins. That was taken away too. I have two young boys. They are beautiful children that my sister and brother-in-law would have been so pleased to spoil. I can only imagine how the children would play and plan their lives together. The injustice is reversed also, for my children. I can only tell them I had a sister who is no longer living. How do I tell them she was murdered trying to protect her children, their cousins? They do not even know they had an uncle and cousins.

You have robbed me of forwarding their (my family's) lives to my children. You have robbed me of telling them of my childhood with my sister and being able to share how I felt about my sister. And of how much I compare our feelings (my sisters and my) and how alike the feelings are with my two boys...so similar to my sister and I. My sister was a person, with a personality of her own, a complex individual. How can you explain in words to someone, especially children, how special someone is and have them understand those feelings. How can you pass along the years of memories I have in my heart that I so want to share but it hurts to tell.

You have robbed me of sharing my brother-in-law, who, to me was the brother I never had. His name has been kept alive in my sons name but I cannot tell him why his name is Patrick for fear of him asking who he was and where he is and entering a line of questions that he is not capable of understanding. Pat was such an individual that I have never met and will never meet again. He protected me and watched over me as a brother. His sense of humor was only second to how mine used to be. We were always one up on another. How it hurts not to be able to tell my children the funny tricks he played on their mother.

You have robbed me of my only niece and nephew, for my sister was the only sibling. How could you take children? How could you snuff out their lives? They should be, at this time, wondering who to date, which college to attend, getting their drivers license, football games, etc. Instead what I have is memories of their innocent eyes, their smiles and laughs, Lisa's plan to master a piano song for Grandpa's birthday, Greg's boyish and mischievous playtime. I see Lisa and Greg's face in my children and only wonder.

You have robbed me of being a good mother. How can my children look to me for protection and the answers when my sister was the perfect mother and she was unable to protect her children and give them reassurance when their cries needed answers?

You have robbed me of my right for privacy and well being. I no longer can go out after dark and drive in my driveway and not be afraid someone is inside waiting for me. How do I feel safe for anyone? I fear for my husband and my children.

Prior to this I was a strong career person. Now I feel stress in more than one pressure at a time. It is hard to juggle my career and still cope with daily life.

You have also robbed me of a good nights rest. I wake at least 5-6 times per night with nightmares, sweats and fright.

I could go into every aspect of my life that has been affected but I respect your intelligence and feel you understand now that I too have been a prisoner in a different sense. Maybe the bars are not physically there but they might as well be. What could have been a great life for me, I have lost.
<u>*The saddest part is I didn't commit the crime but I am paying the punishment*</u>*.*

This punishment will not go away. For every birthday, every holiday, every Jan. 14th, every child and person that resembles my family, every time someone asks do you have any family or where are you from and even when strangers or friends talk of their family, I am thrown into reality and reminders of what could have been and reminders of the hurt. So I live a life (with bars around myself) always on the defensive, always remembering. Again the hurt.

This affected my mother and father. My mother has buried herself into being busy constantly so she won't have to think about her loss. She copes with high blood pressure, stress, asthma, nervousness, bitterness and anger. She copes the best way she knows how. I can never understand how she deals with the loss of a child and grandchildren and a son-in-law. We can't talk about it. It is too close and hurts too much. We try not to talk about it also because she doesn't understand how I cope with the loss of sister, brother-in-law, niece and nephew. The pain is the same but the feelings are different. To a parent, you expect to die before your children. For a sister, you expect to share your life and grow old together.

My father never recovered. He had several heart attacks and suffered from depression. He could not accept his loss and cried daily. He died several years ago a lonely and broken man. What a terrible way to die. He had his last heart attack in October and I watched him go from a 6'3", 180 lb. man to skin and bones. He went into a coma in November and we had to put him in a nursing home. The doctors said in November he would not last for another week and we watched him as he went in and out of a coma. He died at 7:45PM on January 14th, 1989. I feel that is not just coincidental. I feel he either asked my sister to take him with her or the stress of another January 14th was just too much for his body. But I do know he waited.

I cannot even delve into the thousands of friends and family this has affected. I have watched as my uncles and aunts have died from stress and grief. I have watched my friends break down from grief even after so many years and children who knew Lisa and Greg scarred for life. We still get donations for the Gilligan Memorial fund for Drug Abuse and my mother says there are flowers on the gravesite constantly from people and we don't know who.

I can only remember a couple events from the funeral and one is looking from the car behind the hearse and remarking I couldn't see the end of the procession. It was for miles, the bright headlights.

When I started this letter I knew it would be difficult to put into words and in a few pages 12 1/2 years of feelings, but it is important to me for you to know that I have carried this anger, frustration and resentment for too long. I need to speak up. I do not want this to kill me also. I do not want to die from stress and anger. I need to understand. I want to ask questions. It is time for me to try to regain my life and to cope with my loss. If you have remorse, if you have a heart, if you care at all, then will you help me to release these bars around me? I cannot release your bars or let this go unpunished, however, I can learn to possibly forgive and stop wishing you were gone and wishing evil upon you out of the frustration and anger that I feel. If you care, I would think this would matter.

I understand from my mother, talking with your father, that your life has been one of abuse and terrific pain. I am sorry for that. I also understand that you have been through therapy and years of reform school and maybe that was not the perfect environment for a child to grow up. I am again sorry for your misfortune. I understand from your attorney a great deal about your past and the treatment you endured. My only wish is you wouldn't have had to be placed in that situation because we all would not have to be in such a miserable life if your potential could have been reached in a positive fashion instead of negative.

I cannot imagine what death row is like and I cannot imagine what you go through daily with the deaths and memories of what happened on that night in your mind. I cannot change what has happened nor can you. So in turn we are both stuck in limbo and are being punished for the mistakes of one night.

When you stated in your letter that you hope to die for your actions, only you will know if that will make the mistake go away. I know that in your heart you do not want to die or the appeals would have ceased long before now. I cannot change nor can you the outcome.

Please, the only request I ask of you is to help me understand. Questions that have haunted me for these many years. I only ask that you help me give life back to my mother, my friends and living family and myself by answering these questions. I believe what has angered me the most is from all newspaper articles, interviews, etc. there has been no remorse shown on your part. I truly want to forgive but in all these years I have not heard anything but complaints on your surroundings, food, cell mates, etc. Please understand when I hear this my reaction is...my family is in a box 6 feet underground with no options and no life. Why should you be asking for privileges? Help me understand. I have never heard you pass a message through all your attorneys a simple, "I'm sorry". Those simple words would help so much to soften the pain. I have made mistakes in my life and to really mean these words are therapy for me and hopefully help the people to which I have hurt. My last question is the hardest and that is why. I daily ask myself why so brutal, so systematically, so premeditated. Why when I know they were begging for their lives did you just not take the money, jewels and run. Why the children. They would have never recognized you. Was it the drugs, fright,

*what. And why did you beat my brother-in -law so
badly. Was he that much of a threat to you. I don't
understand. As you said in your letter, you have
hours and hours to think about everything but I
don't. I need to raise my children and raise them
with the belief that there is good in everyone and
people really do care. I need to be a good mother
and wife to my husband. I need to be able to open
that part of me I shut down years ago and let my
children and husband inside me. I need to go on
with my life and cope the best way I know. I need to
understand. Please help me.*

Diana Harrington

I waited till the next day, made a copy of my letter
and mailed it to his attorney to forward to Wallace.
I really did not think he would respond.   I thought
to myself at least I said how I felt. Whether he
responds or not, I had been strong enough to tell
him the agony and how the crime he had committed
had affected our lives.

I received an envelope several days later containing
his reply. This letter was among a series of letters

that were sent back and forth. The second letter that I received and several additional letters were some of the most concerning. *They were his confession to the crime.* The entire details of how he had killed my family were detailed in these letters. Each and every word, down to the exact timing, was told and I knew the truth to that evening.

I'm not certain if I believed most of what this criminal said but I did believe his confession. Even until the end, I was never certain of his remorse or his sorrow. I would read his letters that were kind and concerning and then read in the newspapers of his violent hostage taking or his staging a food strike for more prison rights. It was hard to decipher his arrogance from his true feelings so I would take bits and pieces, determine what I could believe and what was fictional.

In fact, he continued his plea of innocence to the public for 25 years. One week before his execution, however, in a public TV interview, he announced that the confession letters he sent to me were true and he indeed had committed the crime. He was guilty.

For 25 years he lied and continued lying right up until the end while telling me the entire story of the crime.

As the years progressed, there were letters sent back and forth with his whines and gripes about the prison system. My response was to ask him to stop griping and do something good for the community or with teens on drugs. I couldn't understand why he would not help others, even though he claimed he had changed. With his superior intelligence he could have written speeches, books, etc. in order to help others. He didn't which frustrated me a great deal. I learned that it was useless to try to appeal to his nature so I switched my efforts to something that I could change.

I was correct in my path to change my efforts from the criminal to something much easier to tackle. I was not adept at understanding a criminal's mind, their actions or persuading them to do something for others.

So was it worth contacting him? Was it worth all
the frustration? Was it worth hearing his lies?

For me, it was worth the correspondence. Not only
did I know the truth of that fateful night and what
actually had happened, I knew I had been able to
vent my feelings. His sorrow and remorse to me
was always implied and secondary so I could not
believe if it was true or fictional.

Needless to say though, had I not taken the first step
in contacting his attorney with my questions, I
would not have had the correspondence throughout
the years. I would never have known the real truth
and the details of that night.

To take a criminal's word, who was a compulsive
liar and sociopath, as the truth is probably naive.
Even if it was implied, a part of me *wanted* to
believe there was an ounce of sorrow from this
criminal. I will never be sure and if I said it doesn't
matter, I would be lying.

I imagine, for all victims of violent crime, we want to believe there is remorse and sorrow for someone who commits such heinous acts. We would like to think to snuff out someone's life without reason is important and especially since they were our loved ones. However, to believe in words without actions is simply something that you can't depend on.

If you want the details to the crime you will never know unless you ask the questions. No one can ever expect or know if the criminal will answer you, or tell you of his guilt. And the answers are not always reliable or accurate… but in certain circumstances, it is well worth the effort to ask.

I have heard from many victims that have contacted their perpetrators. To many the results of what they received were surprising and comforting. For some the details they were searching for were answered. To some they were not. There were victims that were able to forgive the criminal and for some they were able to move on in their lives. Each response is different.

After I wrote the letters I felt as if I had vented and let the perpetrator know my feelings. Even if I had never received a response, I would have felt better putting my feelings on paper. I was always surprised that Wallace wrote back to me, every time I contacted him with my concerns.

You may not have even the remotest wish to contact the criminal. That is entirely your choice and your desires. If you do, however, ask the prosecuting attorney or the criminal's attorney if a contact is available and if they will help you. Possibly they can forward your letters.

I you do not want to contact the perpetrator it is important to recognize your feelings and not keep them inside. Once again, I recommend that you tell someone or write it down. It is important to vent your feelings of how this crime has affected you and how you feel about the situation. Once you have tackled your feelings and let them known it is much easier to move forward.

CHAPTER 7

Dealing with the Media,

Choosing your reporters

Leave me alone! That was my first thought of the media. They clamored for the story and asked questions of how I felt. They wanted to know the history, background or any information I could let them know. They dug and dug, almost relentlessly until they were satisfied, almost more than the investigators of this crime. They invaded my privacy with photos and questions.

The phone continued to ring long after the crime, in fact, for over 25 years the media continued the quest for information. On anniversaries, on appeals, on the criminal's antics and related stories, they continued their contacts. There questions were sometimes insensitive and demanding. Most often, "How did I feel?" and "How was I able to go on?" I could only imagine with questions such as these, they wanted me to fold or completely fall apart.

I only answered questions I felt comfortable answering and at times none at all. I soon began to pick and choose who I would let interview me and chose the questions that would be asked. I wanted factual questions on the case, the process, my family and certain aspects of the crime. As mentioned, there was a small handful that I actually felt comfortable talking with about these delicate topics.

I learned quickly, however, that a large percent of the reporters were sincerely interested in teaching the public about my family, their lives and to tell the correct, accurate story of this crime. There was a large majority that wanted to inform the public of the long drawn out appeals process, the antics of this criminal from death row, what was happening in the prosecution of this person and to compare this case with other cases.

These journalists were trying to do their jobs and in order for them to do a good job they needed to poke and probe. I developed, in the years after the initial crime, a bonding with some journalists. A friendship that cannot compare to any relationships I have, ever had or will have. These people wrote, reported and interviewed from the heart. They were as involved with the story as I was. They could relate to their loved ones being gone and if they were in this circumstance, how they would react. Their stories reflected this passion for realistic reporting.

They understood the frustrations with the government, the criminal and the length of time it took to find out any new information with the progress of the case.

I, in turn, was determined to make sure every time this case or criminal was mentioned, my family received equal time. They knew my goal. I wanted to make sure the public did not forget the horrendous crime that had occurred nor forget the victims of this violent crime. This was simple to share my intentions with many of these reporters but difficult with others.

The sympathetic reporters instinctively understood my plight. They also were on a mission to inform the public of the advances in the case. They understood that the entire story was not about the criminal but about the crime and victims.

In fact, I most often received more information from the media than I did from the justice system. The only time I received any information from the Governors office was a couple weeks before the execution.

The reporters and I both shook our heads in disbelief each time a new appeal would begin, or when a new attorney was presented the case. I believe the longest wait for any progress was when the case sat on a judge's desk awaiting any decision. Reports of the delays were focused on the procrastination of the system and the frustration it had on the victims.

I was not the only victim. The entire community were victims. They waited for any news of the case, good or bad; informative or just repetition. They thirsted for information as I did. It was the job of these reporters to furnish that information to us.

The small percent of reporters that were sensationalists and media seekers made my life a living nightmare. They asked questions that crossed the line, invaded my privacy and insulted my intelligence. A story to them was to try and make me cry. Tears, it seemed, made news and made the story credible.

They are easily turned off if you refuse to comment. You only need to remember, you are the story and you make the story.   If they do not receive an answer, there is nothing to report or write about. My Mother had the right idea. When things got tough she would take the phone off the hook and become invisible.

Become adept at picking and choosing the reporters you want to talk with. There are certain ones who will be sympathetic to your feelings and they will respect your family over the criminal. With these you will be allowed to talk about the crime, your family and your opinions as first and foremost with the criminal being secondary.

CHAPTER 8

Looking for a Therapist,

"Do I Really Need One?"

The brain is a wonderful instrument. It offers
memory loss when you are in shock. It offers the
repetition of daily chores and motions so we can
accomplish them without thinking. Shock is what
most victims undergo with the initial news of the
crime. A type of denial until you can accept the
truth and loss. I believe your body goes on
automatic pilot and it automatically does what
needs to be accomplished throughout the days after
the crime.

When the shock wore off and the memories of what
had happened started flooding in my brain, it was
more than I could handle. I forgot a big portion of
what I actually did and what happened over a period
of several years. I went about the motions of
everyday life, going to work, continuing my career,
raising the kids, being a wife, grocery shopping, etc.
But in reality that is all I did...make the motions.

Finding help is easier said than done but a good therapist/doctor is sometimes necessary in order to find comfort from your pain and learn to cope from day to day.

Back in the 1980's, it was hard to find grief counseling groups. However, I still searched for group sessions that I could join but with not much luck. I thought they might be able to share some insights as to what was happening to me. I basically knew why I was stressed out, why parts of my memory were blocked and why I was so sad. I wanted to be able to handle the day to day life and cope with this tragedy in my life. For me, these group sessions were of little help.

I have found today though, there are wonderful groups from grief, violent crime to stress counseling that are available. Almost every hospital or doctor can direct you to a session that can be extremely helpful. Pick one that is most helpful to you.

With the lack of group counseling and still needing some guidance, I decided to look for a Psychiatrist,

Therapist or Psychologist. For myself, I felt a
Psychiatrist would be more helpful. A Psychiatrist
is a Doctor of Psychology and they are able to
prescribe drugs such as antidepressants,
tranquilizers, etc. if needed for depression, anxiety
or nerves.

Now to find one! I wasn't going to stop until I
found the perfect doctor. I wanted to feel
comfortable talking with them but most of all I
wanted to trust them with my feelings.

I visited several before finally finding the one that I
felt could help me the most.

Each appointment started the same way. I would
begin by with, "I am having problems, my only
sister, brother in law, 5 yr old niece and 4 yr old
nephew were murdered when they walked into their
home and surprised a burglar. They were all tied up
and shot in the head. The man that killed them is on
death row and is now in the 5th year of appeals. I
have had to endure the funeral, trial and years of
pain. I want to be able to cope with this on a day to

day basis."

The look on some of their faces as I finished were almost as white and sickly as when I had found out the night of the murders. They didn't know what to say. One even said that the crime was horrible and he would have had difficulty coping. If he couldn't handle it.... how was he going to help me! Immediately I knew these were not the right doctors for me.

I finally heard what I needed to hear. A doctor that said the magic words, "I am so sorry, I imagine it has been a very trying ordeal for you. You will never forget this crime nor will you ever forget the way you loved and love your family but we can try to diminish the stress. We'll take it day by day".

It was exactly what I wanted to hear. I didn't want to go through all the details, all the anger and all the pain. I just wanted to hear someone say I was going to be able to live day by day and that I would be all right.

Just as in any profession, I'm sure there are
Psychiatrists, Psychologists and Therapists that
specialize in certain fields or are better at certain
therapy. Try to find one that is adept at violent
crime, grief or stress. Find out how they will deal
with your feelings and questions.

Life after violent crime will never be the same but
with competent medical help; you can learn to live
one day at a time. You can learn to control the
crime and the pain and not let them control you.

My Psychiatrist has prescribed drugs when I needed
them and has provided a therapist who taught me
meditation along with relaxing techniques. She
helped me with my memory and deciphered my
nightmares.

Over the years I returned when I felt the need for
counseling or was going through a rough period. All
in all, I have found her advice and professional
expertise extremely helpful in coping with such a
tragedy.

From experience, continue to look for help. It is out there. After going to and leaving several psychiatrists, therapists and group sessions, I finally found the one that had the answer to my question…How can I go on?

Don't just look in the yellow pages for a doctor, do some research first. Ask your general doctor if he knows of a good grief or stress Therapist or Psychologist/Psychiatrist. He probably knows you best and can recommend the correct therapist for you.

Along with a good doctor for the mind, don't forget a good doctor for your body. Stress and anxiety can cause aches and pains you never thought were imaginable.

I lost an enormous amount of weight after the crime. I just did not feel like eating nor did I remember to eat. Eating properly, even when you don't feel like it, is very important. The body uses B and C vitamins to cope with continuous stress. It is very essential to get enough of these vitamins, along with plenty of rest.

Exercise is equally as important as food and rest.
Exercise produces endorphins which are feel good
hormones in your body. They have been known to
relieve anxiety. Any exercise such as a walking in
the park or with your pet, riding your bike or going
to the mall for a leisurely stroll will not only get
your mind off of bad thoughts but the change in
scenery will be good for you. You might not feel
like it after the crime but it is important that you
have time away from your grief and let your mind
rest.

You might want to ask your doctor for an exercise
program to help relieve your stress.

I'm sure eating and exercising is the furthest thing
from your mind but it is important for your overall
well being. It is also necessary for the long term
healing of your body and soul.

CHAPTER 9

Your Best Friend May Be your Pet

After a violent crime it is literally impossible to talk about your loved ones or the crime without crying, breaking down or hurting too much to talk about it. It is very easy to get into a habit of running away from the thought of talking to people not only about the crime and your loved one but sometimes just normal conversations.

Whenever you talk, the thoughts of your loved ones being gone, how they died and the circumstances surrounding their deaths is unbearable. Others do not understand that through simple and polite conversations they ask questions that make you uncomfortable. From this friendliness, curiosity and their need to know details, it only drives you further and further away from talking.

Sometimes it is as simple as not wanting anyone to give you advice. You want no backtalk and you just want to vent. You might want to ramble on with no intent of anyone giving you critique or answers.

I can't tell you how many times my little dog helped me through the rough days. I would talk to her in words that I couldn't say to people. I could tell her how I felt and she never judged, spoke back or refused to listen. I could tell her how much I hurt and how much I missed my family. She would let me tell my stories over and over and she would never say she was tired of listening to them. Many times I would sit there holding her little head and being wrapped up in the moment and she never complained.

She would look at me, with her puppy dog eyes, as if she knew each and every word spoken and each and every feeling I felt. She had an uncanny ability to sense just when I needed her to snuggle up against me and give me her "best friend" hugs and kisses.

A pet can sometimes open the door for your own conversations and feelings to flow to others. Many times I would tell my pet my darkest feelings first and then later I could reveal them to my husband. After I heard the words being uttered from my lips, they somehow did not feel as bad or hurt as bad the second time around.

Whether it is a dog, cat, bird, turtle, fish or whatever, I think the need for that unconditional love and attention is something that is needed by any victim. It is not only a proven stress reliever, blood pressure reducer and promotes exercise but it is also a proven fact a pet can reduce depression, a major health risk and a normal response to violent crime.

A pet can also offer you the safety and security that you need. After a violent crime, your world can appear shaky and you feel danger is all around you. Even the smallest dogs and even cats can be protection and make your world more comfortable.

My real point in this chapter is…whoever you talk to, make sure you talk. I'm sure you won't feel at ease talking to the local grocery store clerk but sometimes the people you least expect can be the best avenues for discussion.

I went for years not wanting to talk about my sister, brother-in-law, niece and nephew. I held their memories deep inside me and would not share them with anyone. It hurt to talk about them and in turn I missed out on keeping them alive with other people.

I was afraid that people would ask where they were or what happened and I would have to relive the crime and how they were killed. I sometimes felt I was on pins and needles with everyone, waiting for them to ask questions about my family.

I missed out on many friendships and relationships just because I didn't want to get that close to anyone and I didn't want to get into a situation where I would have to talk about the crime.

Once I started sharing stories and talking about these my beautiful family, I started to make them come alive in my heart again and make them alive to other people.

I went for years not realizing that others were satisfied with my answers to their questions of "what happened?" with a simple, "I'm not ready to talk about it yet," or "It is very complicated and it hurts a great deal to talk about it". They were fine and would go to other conversations.

Once I started to share my stories of Pat turning on my windshield wipers, blaring my radio and putting my seat back to recline when I got into my car because he wanted to teach me a lesson to lock my car doors. They got a clear picture of his humor and protectiveness of me. When I shared my sister's love of cooking, playing piano and her constantly being involved with church, school and other projects, they knew what a lovely caring person she was.

When I started talking about my family I realized not only what I missed but also what I had. I felt I was so blessed to have them as my family members and to share them with others made me feel even luckier.

Yes, there are things that will hurt when you talk about your loved ones but the more you talk about them the easier it is to continue and share. The stories will make you smile again.

Do not focus on your loss, focus on how much you still have, their memories. No one can take that from you. As long as you keep them alive, they will stay alive. Don't keep your emotions or your words bottled up inside.

Learn to share and talk about your feelings, loved one's and tell the stories. If at first it is told to your pet, great…when you are ready you will be able to share your stories with others.

CHAPTER 10...

"What is closure? When Will I Heal?"

On the day of the execution I wondered, "What would I do? "Where would I go?" "How would I feel?"   It had been 25 years but I never thought of what I would do or how I would feel about this day.

Would this day be the end of 25 years of this heinous crime breathing down my neck? Yes, it was true that I would no longer have to "put up" with the system. I would no longer be a victim of this criminal's antics from death row. The fight to keep my family first and the criminal second would end and the never ending roller coaster of appeals would cease. However, would it give me peace? Was this day actually what I was waiting for?

For 25 years the word "closure" was always spoken simultaneously with "the execution". Some thought this execution would finally bring closure, an end to the suffering. Justice for the taking of 4 innocent lives would be served. This execution would finally bring peace and a mind set of tranquility along with closure.

However, it was not the execution that would bring these feelings. It was not the death of a criminal, another human being that would bring the salve to soothe all wounds. So if it wasn't waiting for the execution that held me in limbo, what would bring me some peace? What would bring "closure"?

My husband said it very simply and very briefly, "As long as someone can remember the crime and remember their loved ones, there will never be closure." An execution will never bring closure. The ending of another's life does not bring closure for another's.

Don't understand me incorrectly, I am neither for nor against the death penalty. That is each person's individual opinion. I am only stating that an execution does not bring closure for victims. The only closure that an execution brings is the closure on a chapter of one's life and the opening of another one. The next chapter in my life, after 25 years, was to move to the next plateau in the healing process.

On the eve of the execution, I planned a prayer service for the community, family and friends and myself.

It was perfectly clear that this was not a prayer service for the criminal's execution. It really had nothing to do with the execution. It was a continuance of the healing process for the community and myself.

There are so many people that are stuck in the moment of the crime and never move forward to a place where they can remember the happy times, the smiles and the sharing of the victim's lives. I think that the severe shock of the crime halts that healing process to a degree. After so many years the wounds are still open for many.

As we go through years without moving, we are the ones that are cheated out of our loved ones memories. Instead of celebrating their lives we only feel and remember how they died and not how they lived. Letting yourself remember their lives and how they lived continues the healing in yourself.

These words are from the prayer service. Hopefully they will help you heal as they helped me move to the next plateau...

To every thing there is a season, and a time to every purpose under the heaven:
A time to be born, and a time to die; a time to plant, and a time to pluck up that which is planted;
A time to kill, and a time to heal; a time to break down, and a time to build up;
A time to weep, and a time to laugh; a time to mourn, and a time to dance;
A time to cast away stones, and a time to gather stones together; a time to embrace, and a time to refrain from embracing;
A time to get, and a time to lose; a time to keep, and a time to cast away;
A time to rend, and a time to sew; a time to keep silence, and a time to speak;
A time to love, and a time to hate; a time of war,

and a time of peace.

...to everything there is a time...

It is now a time for healing....There have been many tears, heartaches and loneliness that have followed us.

We are all too familiar with our tremendous loss. Our hearts are broken and the pain is unbearable.

I am reminded of a passage from a poem....**"What though the radiance which was once so bright be now forever taken from my sight...I will grieve not...rather find strength in what remains behind...."**

It is now a time to bind and soothe the wounds that are present.

It is now a time for healing....with healing there is a time for smiling and remembering. It is a time to remember with love and fond memories all the people that are no longer with us.

It is our memory of what made these people

important to us...of the shared love, laughter, kindness and triumphs that preserve their life within us. It is a gift they left us and one we should nurture and never forget. When we start to talk about our wonderful memories, share our feelings and support each other, we will begin the process of healing. We can begin to shed the unhappiness...and focus on their presence in our hearts and in our minds. They were and are a part of us...a part that will be with us as long as we remember. They will never be gone; they will always be here in spirit.

There is also a time to weep and a time to laugh. We all have cried and wept over those tragically taken from us. Our sorrow and our sadness have long been felt. With healing there is a time to weep no more. It is a time to dry our tears. It is a time to laugh and a time to smile.

There is a time to put the love back in our hearts. Anger and hatred have no room in a heart filled with love, understanding, compassion and happiness. To reach out to the ones we love. To thank God for the time we have with one another.

There is a time to enjoy life... that time is now. To cherish every second we are alive. A time to watch with anticipation every sunrise and every sunset.

There is also a time for spiritual guidance. A time to pray and a time to ask for help. To ask God for his continued support and for his help in healing. Now is the time to trust in our faith and draw on the warm and loving memories that brought us so much joy.

We are asking for a lot...we are asking for a time to smile, a time to love, a time to laugh, a time to live and a time to heal. We have a long way to go...but our memories will ease that journey............

Maybe for you this healing will take 5 years, 10 years or maybe 25 years. Whatever time passes, I hope you will reach this plateau where you celebrate the lives of your loved ones and the memories are fond, happy memories that make you smile and laugh.

CHAPTER 11

A Letter to the Senator, Governor, Media...

This is the letter I wrote to the Senator, Governor and the media the morning after the execution....

March 10, 2005

I woke up this morning, March 10th, to a beautiful sunrise. The sun was bright and clear and I thanked God I was viewing it. I then remembered the passage that I had read at the prayer service for my family.... ***"One day at a time..This is enough. Do not look back and grieve over the past for it is gone: and do not be troubled about the future, for it has not yet come.***
Live in the present, and make it so beautiful it will be worth remembering".

I was then saddened by the thought that there was a father that had just lost his son and sisters that had just lost their brother. It was a strange feeling but I did realize that what I had said for years was absolutely true. I did not hate Donald Wallace but I hated the crime he committed and despised the situation he had caused and I was angry about his years and years of media coverage and antics. I felt it completely unfair the sorrow, agony and pain that was placed on so many hearts.

Am I a believer in the death penalty... no. Am I convinced the death penalty is wrong.... no. I am convinced that heinous crimes should have quick and speedy punishment. The crime and loss of loved ones is enough agony that one should bear, much less the constant reminders of the criminal's appeals, protests and constant complaints of his rights and living conditions.

I am totally convinced that when a person has been proven guilty beyond a reasonable doubt that the rights of the criminal should be forever taken away. There was never any doubt that this person was guilty. He not only was sentenced in a court of law but confessed to the brutal crime. Guilt was never an issue. The appeals should have ceased, the rights should have ceased. It is definitely not inhumane to receive meals, medical attention, dental visits, counseling, clean clothes, warm surroundings and an education that is far superior then what is available for many of the average person.

As in a Childs punishment, time out is for sitting on a chair and reflecting what they did wrong. It is not an occasion to debate if the chair is too hard, or if the child should receive snacks or breaks when the punishment is being enforced. It is punishment.

In the same respect, when a prisoner has been sentenced to incarceration it is not permission for them to take the podium and to protest for additional rights, more TV, free phone calls, more comfortable living conditions and better food. It is a time to reflect on whatever crime they have committed.

I find it hard to believe anyone on death row could find rehabilitation and find it even more difficult to imagine these criminals back on the streets. Even as I heard Donald Wallace talk of his belief in God and his belief in not harming anyone, my trust level was not comfortable to even suggest putting him into the same situation as 25 years ago. What would the statistics be whether he would run away this time or simply fight and kill again? His track record was not good before this crime and certainly did not improve with the killing of four innocent people.

Do I have the answers.... no, I am just a victim. However, I am a victim with a voice. I am a victim that has endured too much pain, suffering and will never find closure in this man's death but will find closure in the memories of my family.

I am by no means the only victim of violent crime. There are thousands and thousands of victims in the world. We do have one voice however, and that voice is change.

Change in a system. A system that eventually proves that crime doesn't pay but what is the debt victims pay in order to arrive at the correct conclusion. I ask the Governor, the State of Indiana and the Victims of Violent Crime to speak out. I also ask

the pro death penalty and anti death penalty
advocates to speak out. Instead of the millions
spent on criminals, there should be a time limit on
appeals, there should be a final decision if the
death penalty should be carried out or not enforced,
there should be a victims relief program not with
any statutes and not with the enormous and
ridiculous set of rules and regulations in order to
qualify. There should be a victim's relief for years
of support for the victims that endure anger,
suffering, sadness and financial distress.

The burden for the cost of the penal system and any
victim's relief should come from a self sustaining
correctional process. It should not be unreasonable
or any violation of anyone's' rights, but a
reasonable expectation, that incarcerated criminals
be sufficiently productive to support the
correctional facility, as well as, to provide relief to
the victims, child support, etc.. This would end the
victims and the taxpayer's burden of supporting
criminals over the many years of prison life.
Perhaps it would be a greater deterrent to crime if a
person knew they would be forced to work and not

be allowed to keep the monies that they had earned...the price of their crime would then have a face.

*There should be in <u>no way</u> the criminal's name remembered and the victims name pushed aside. It should **always be the victims first** and **the crime remembered** rather than the perpetrator.*

Sincerely, Diana & Ted Harrington, Sister of Theresa Gilligan

ADDITION...

PREVIEW OF THE BOOK.....

SURVIVING THE DEATH PENALTY....

by Diana & Ted Harrington

PRELUDE....Wednesday, March 9, 2005

It was 11:30AM as we slowly drove down the narrow winding road at St. Joseph's Cemetery in Evansville, Indiana. I thought to myself how much the cemetery had grown and how many monuments were new to this section. The stones recorded history going back several hundred years and yet there were monuments with dates as recent as 2005. A sadness prevailed, as I'm sure it had for countless others, when looking to the nearly full hillside.

We stopped the car at the familiar site and I opened the door. I took a deep breath as I had each time I visited. It was as overwhelming at that moment as it had been 25 years ago. The pain was as fresh as it had been on January 14th, 1980. My heart once again was beating fast and my body was beginning to tremble.

We walked under the large oak tree that had grown tall, full and stately in the many years since I first came here. I approached the third row, third marker from the left with the same sense of loss as I had every previous time.

There was a large double monument inscribed,

DOROTHY JAMES SAHM....
OCTOBER 26, 1920 - AUGUST 1, 1999
&
LAWRENCE A SAHM....
MAY 1, 1920 - JANUARY 14, 1989

My Dad and Mom. I missed them and anguished over how much they had suffered after that fateful day in January, 1980.

Would today be the end that had started with one insane moment? That brief instant in time that had changed their lives, my life and the lives of so many. It was too late for them but would it be the end to my suffering?

My parents were not vengeful people but had waited so long for justice and an end to so many years of living each day with the pain of this tragedy. Not that there would have ever been closure for them but they died without an apology or seeing any remorse from the criminal that had changed their world.

I had watched how my Dad went from a vivacious active man, full of life, love and humor to a lonely sad man that died exactly nine years, to the day, of the crime that claimed his eldest daughter. He had been ill for some months leading up to the 14th of January in 1989. I believe he simply allowed himself to die on that ninth anniversary when so much of his life and those he loved were destroyed. He had never been able to reconcile himself to the loss and began the slow descent leading to this day when his heart could no longer accept the emptiness of loss. Some thought it ironic, bizarre or miraculous, depending on whom you spoke with, that Dad passed away on that exact anniversary date. I think it was what he wanted most. I think he finally found the peace he deserved.

I also watched my Mom, a wonderful lady with such drive, ambition; energy and kindness become one of the strongest women I had ever met. She looked to God and never lost faith. Holding her head high for years, while inside, I knew she had pain so unbearable that she uttered the word "Why ?" on her deathbed and " Not yet ! " I knew what she was asking but I did not have the answers that might bring her peace nor was I able to give strength to a heart that had suffered too much.

They were victims of a crime. If you look at their death certificates you will find that they died of natural causes. That they died of broken hearts speaks to the real truth of their deaths.

I said a quiet prayer and told them I loved them dearly.

I moved just a step away, to the right from their gravesite to a larger monument. The silk flowers were looking quite ragged from the long winter and there were several cards neatly laid along the side of the monument.

The name **GILLIGAN** was inscribed along the top portion with lovely engraved cascading flowers and vines on each of the sloping sides. The name had been chiseled across the entire length of the monument. It was large and bold, suggesting a special memorial to someone equally special.

Under the name **GILLIGAN** was an engraved circle in the shape of a plate with deep-set rims. There were two delicate doves in the middle, detailed and drawn together as one. The artistry was compelling and drew you to the image. On the bottom rim of the circle were two intertwined wedding rings and at the top of the circle was

Chiseled in lovely script lettering, **"WE ARE ONE LOVE FOREVER"**. When I read the inscription it had such deep meaning and spoke the greatest truth of those resting beneath the shadow of the stone. I remembered the first time I saw this plate and knew later it was the perfect eulogy for the monument.

Under the circle, to the left read:

Gregory P.

Sept. 25, 1975

Jan. 14, 1980

To the right was:

G. Patrick

Apr. 10, 1949

Jan. 14, 1980

Next was:

Theresa Sahm

Oct. 5, 1949

Jan. 14, 1980

And at the end was:

Lisa Lynne

May 6, 1974

Jan 14, 1980

My family…. My sister, brother-in-law, niece and nephew.

Words still could not explain the feelings, the depth of loss, the pain of remembering, even after all these years.

I thought what a long time it had been. However, even today, I can close my eyes and feel as if the clock had been turned back 25 years. The sadness, the emptiness in my heart and the agony had always been there, the same over all these years. Would today be different?

This evening, or actually at 12:01am, March 10, 2005, a drug infused execution was to take place in Michigan City, Indiana. It would end the life of Donald Ray Wallace Jr., the person who had brutally murdered four innocent people. Wallace had tied all four with a cord, tortured them, beat my brother-in-law with barbells and fired six fatal shots to their heads execution style at close range They were my thirty year old sister and brother-in-law, Theresa and Pat, my niece Lisa , five years old and my four year old nephew, Greg.

I shook my head in disbelief. After years of denial, he now claimed "It happened in an instant. A brief moment of insanity," I wondered...how anyone could have committed such a senseless and callous murder...not once...but four times?"

He had brought his own gun with him to ensure the success of his crime. He purposely, and with careful

thought, willfully decided in that moment to execute
these people in an effort to escape the consequences
of a burglary. The community and I came to see
him as a compulsive liar, a diagnosed sociopath and
a mass murderer.

He had claimed his innocence to this crime. He had
blamed accomplices and never took responsibility
for his actions. However, I knew for over twelve
years that he had been the only killer. He had
confessed in letters to me the real chain of events
leading to the last moments of what happened that
night. Yes, he had confessed the entire crime to me
while denying to the world his involvement.

As I stood at my family's graves, I felt a renewed
anger that the week before his scheduled execution,
he made a pubic confession. Why had he waited 25
years? Would tonight's execution quench this new
anger?

Was it worth killing still another person? I had
already been told I would not and could not make
this stop. Why would I expect my words to make

any difference today? Over the entire 25 years, my voice was deaf to everyone's ears.

My mission was to make everyone remember the crime, the victims and the brutality of the crime but Wallace was always in the forefront. The protests, hostage taking, hunger strikes, trial, appeals, feigning insanity..... It never stopped.

No matter how much I tried to convince people that it wasn't the criminal that should be heard but the victims, no one took action. Wallace still got his way. He manipulated and orchestrated the system from Death Row and used it to his advantage at every opportunity. I wanted him to just go away. Maybe I would have thought differently today had it not been such a rebellious 25 years or if I did not have to deal with him. Did I really hate him so much to want him dead? I had always said it was what he did and the situation I hated and not Donald Ray Wallace Jr. Was that true?

It had been such a long time and the journey had been an unbelievable nightmare of highs and lows.

The highs too shallow and the lows a frightening depth to climb above. In this cold brisk March wind, I distinctly remembered all the strange and incredible paths my life had taken. Would that stop tonight or would there be a continuance to this past?

All I knew was I was in the right place right now....with those I had loved and those that had loved me.

I was in Evansville, Indiana, not Michigan City, as Donald Wallace approached his end. I too, was ending a chapter in my life. I was with all the people that had stood by my family and me for 25 years. Tonight we would be gathered at Saint Theresa's Church for a prayer vigil, for the entire city, to remember the lives of my sister and her family. Tonight was for everyone who had suffered from this crime. We would pray for strength, guidance and support. We would start the healing process and maybe, for some, find an end to a long ordeal.

This was not a night of prayers for Donald Wallace Jr... Tonight was a night to remember the victims and their lives. I had no answers nor was I sure that tomorrow would hold any answers. But right here, right now, I was in the right place.

Chapter 1

January 1980…

I always adored and admired Theresa, my only sister. Theresa was older than me by two………….

The Gilligan Family

Patrick, Theresa, Lisa & Gregory

Surviving the Death Penalty...

The true story of one of the most heinous
crimes committed in Indiana
the crime, the criminal, the victims
and the unrest this death penalty wait
held for 25 years.

By Diana & Ted Harrington

Donald
Ray
Wallace
Jr.

The true story of one of the most heinous crimes committed in Indiana...the Patrick Gilligan Family... The crime, the criminal Donald Ray Wallace Jr., the victims and the unrest this death penalty wait held for 25 years. It is a parallel story of both the criminal, the victims and their lives. This story is not only about a cold blooded crime, but also about the journey one travels as a victim. This is the story from the initial crime to its conclusion, with twists & turns that most average people seldom understand or endure. This book tells of the Death Penalty wait for both the criminal and the victims and how their lives are forever intertwined. Stories such as this one are few and far between. Crimes happen in the millions but the victim's story, along with the criminal's story, are often not told in their entirety.

AUTHORS BIO:

Diana & Ted Harrington reside in Kentucky with their two college sons. They have participated in many newspaper and TV interviews, as well as, PBS talk shows. This case has been widely televised and reported nationwide with excerpts from interviews and opinions

They have recently published their book; *Surviving the Death Penalty*...Diana's credentials include published articles, editorials, poems and letters, over the past 25 years, in all forms of media. She has recently been recognized for her letters to **NOVA and VOCA** in June 2005. **Anne Seymour**, from the **U.S. Justice Department**, read the letters on her behalf at the **National Organization for Victims Assistance** in **Washington DC** Forum for Congressmen and Senators.

Diana has been a featured writer in the **Crime Victims' Report,** a publication for **Criminal Justice Professionals** and **providers of Support Services**. This is the largest journal-type newsletter in this field.

She continues to challenge the government on **The Appeals Process** and the **Victims of Crime Act (VOCA).**

The Gilligan Family,
Theresa, Lisa, Patrick and Gregory

www.ingramcontent.com/pod-product-compliance
Lightning Source LLC
Chambersburg PA
CBHW032008040426
42448CB00006B/534